D1062990

The Spirit and the Word

Revell Books
By Robert E. Coleman

The Master Plan of Evangelism
Dry Bones Can Live Again
One Divine Moment (Edited by)
Written in Blood
Established by the Word (Revised Edition)
Life in the Living Word (Revised Edition)
The Spirit and the Word (Revised Edition)

THE SPIRIT

and

THE WORD

Bible Lessons for
Spirit-Filled Christians

Revised Edition

Robert E. Coleman

SPIRE BOOKS

FLEMING H. REVELL COMPANY
OLD TAPPAN, NEW JERSEY

Scripture references in this book are from the King James Version of the Bible.

140,000 copies in print in English editions
Used Around the World
This book is translated with permission by a number of missionary societies and national churches in the languages of Arabic, Cinyanja, Ilocano, Kanarese, Kapauku, Kipsigis, Korean, Kui, Neo-Melanesian, Ponapean, Quiche, Shona, Spanish, and Zulu.

ISBN 0-8007-8192-9
Copyright © 1965, 1969, 1975 by Robert E. Coleman
Published by Fleming H. Revell Company
Library of Congress Catalog Card Number: 75-5208
All Rights Reserved
Printed in the United States of America

CONTENTS

INTRODUCTION

PLUS POWER

It has been said that many machines have been invented which can do the work of a hundred ordinary men, but that no machine has ever been invented which can do the work of just one extraordinary man.

How true! There simply is no substitute for excellence. Men may try to get by on less, sometimes performing so well that the compromise looks like the real thing, but the difference is still there, and in the time of testing it will be discovered.

Unfortunately, this spirit of compromise has invaded the church. Many people through human striving are trying valiantly to do a job that can only be done in the power of the Holy Spirit. The resultant form of religion may meet the ordinary standards of church respectability, and even give a sense of personal security and contentment, but it cannot alter the gnawing realization of spiritual powerlessness. There is no radiance in the life. No thrill in the soul. The wonderful strength and joy of the believer at conversion may still be there to assure the heart, but still the Christian wants something more.

There can be no doubt that the New Testament church living in the glow of Pentecost had something more. Anyone reading the Book of Acts can see by comparison with the present church that the early Christians had something in their lives which gave to them an extraordinary power.

VARIOUSLY DEFINED

But is this kind of life available to every child of God today? If so, what is it, and how can it be obtained?

At this point, many conflicting answers are given. Perhaps this is good, for we are thus made aware that the ways of God are greater than any interpretation of them, and regardless of the position taken, there will be much more for all of us to learn. We would therefore be wise not to insist that everyone see this new life as we do. Another point of view might correct a blind spot in our vision. In humility, recognizing our limited understanding, we would all do well to seek a greater insight into the truth by sharing with each other.

Yet, interestingly enough, when we get through our differences, we become aware that a remarkable number of men and women greatly used of God, from various schools of thought, witness to essentially the same kind of plus experience in their own lives. Naturally, they speak of this experience in different ways, depending upon their particular doctrinal point of view. Some call it "full salvation," "perfect love," or "the victorious life." Others may prefer to describe it as "the baptism of the Holy Spirit," "the rest of faith," "death to self," or something else. The terminology, however, is not the important thing. What is significant is that there exists among Christian leaders representing many different theological and church connections a basic unanimity of agreement upon the fact— the fact of a deeper and abiding life in Christ that is normally realized subsequent to regeneration when the trusting heart is delivered from the bondage of self, filled with the Holy Spirit, and set aflame by the love of God to serve the Lord with gladness.

This is the experience, however it may be defined, which characterized the early church. It is the dynamic life which has sustained the witness of the redeemed amid the pressures of this world throughout the ages. It is still the power that fills the lives of many Christians today, and, indeed, by the grace of God, it is the privilege of us all.

IS IT SCRIPTURAL?

But our confidence must rest upon more than the witness of men. Personal testimony, though convincing, is not infallible. That is why ultimately all experience must be measured by the Word of God, the Holy Scripture, the only final authority for our faith. What we believe by experience must be attested by the Bible or it is not reliable.

This little book has been prepared to help you at this point. As such, it is a sequel to the Bible studies entitled *Established by the Word* and *Life in the Living Word.* Since these first lessons deal more with the initial work of the Spirit in Christian experience, normally the student will want to have completed them before undertaking this study. However, this book is designed as a unit in itself, and can be used by anyone sincerely seeking to find for himself answers in the Bible to some of the questions pertaining to the Spirit-filled life.

The brief compass of the book naturally requires considerable selection in the topics chosen for study. Not every interesting facet of this subject can be treated. But an attempt has been made to deal constructively with matters which are immediately apparent to the person entering the experience.

Our purpose throughout is to get beyond terminology to the truth and the personal application of it. Until this has been done, in fact, the Scripture has not been rightly divided. The Bible is not written to stimulate theological discussion, but to change men's lives, and when its redeeming message is understood and applied to life by the Holy Spirit, that is exactly what happens.

It is hoped that you will keep this uppermost in your mind as you use this book. Be honest with yourself. And as you seek to apply your heart to the truth, you may be assured that your faith does not stand in the wisdom of men, but in the power of God.

Sanctify them through Thy truth:
Thy Word is truth.
—John 17:17

HOW TO USE THIS BOOK

In Your Personal Study

1. Use this book along with your Bible.

2. Read carefully the introduction to each lesson.

3. Study a few questions every day. Be regular. Develop a habit of Bible study.

4. After reading the question, look up the Scripture reference. Where only a verse or two are listed, it would be helpful to read the whole paragraph of which the reference is a part.

5. Pray that God will lead you to find the truth in each Scripture.

6. Think on the verse long enough to understand clearly what it says, then determine what it means to you.

7. Write very briefly the answer to the question in your own words. Be yourself. Try not to copy the Bible answer word for word.

8. Write your personal application at the end of each lesson.

9. Memorize the Scripture verses in connection with each lesson.

10. Take any unanswered questions in your mind to your pastor or counselor. This experienced advisor can then review your progress and give you further instruction.

In Group Study

The procedure is the same as that outlined for the individual, except that the completed lessons are discussed among the members of the group in meeting together. Thus the group itself assumes the place of the pastor or counselor in reviewing the work and in making additional assignments.

WORDS FOR REFLECTION . . .

The fullness of God is in Christ, and Christ lives in men through His Spirit. He is Himself the gift. He brings all the blessings of grace, and Wisdom, and Power, but He is the Blesser and the Blessing. There is in the soul a very true sense of a divinely real Presence. The Spirit makes the Presence real. This is the crowning mystery and glory of Grace. The Christian religion is not a set of doctrines about Christ, neither is it a rule of life based on the teaching and example of Christ. It is not even an earnest and sincere endeavour to live according to the mind and spirit of Christ. It is Life, and that Life is the Life of Christ. It is a continuation of the Life of the Risen Lord in His Body which is the Church, and in the sanctified believer. "Christ liveth in me" is the essence of the Christian religion as set forth in the New Testament. It is not a system, but a Presence; the Spirit of Christ indwelling the spirit of man.

SAMUEL CHADWICK

I will mediate and be still, until something of the overwhelming glory of the truth fall upon me, and faith begin to realize it: I am His Temple, and in the secret place He sits upon the throne. . . . I do now tremblingly accept the blessed truth: God the Spirit; the Holy Spirit; Who is God Almighty dwells in me. O my Father, reveal within me what it means, lest I sin against Thee by saying it and not living it.

ANDREW MURRAY

Suppose we saw an army sitting down before a granite fort, and they told us that they intended to batter it down. We might ask them, "How?" They point to a cannon ball. Well, but there is no power in that; it is heavy, but not more than half a hundred, or perhaps a hundred weight. If all the men in the army hurled it against the fort, they would make no impression. They say; "No; but look at the cannon." Well, there is no power in that. A child may ride upon it, a bird may perch in its mouth; it is a machine, and nothing more. "But look at the powder." Well, there is no power in that; a child may spill it, a sparrow may peck it. Yet this powerless powder and powerless ball are put into the powerless cannon; one spark of fire enters it; and then, in the twinkling of an eye, that powder is a flash of lightning, and that ball a thunderbolt, which smites as if it had been sent from heaven. So it is with our church machinery at this day: we have all the instruments necessary for pulling down strongholds, and Oh for a baptism of fire!

WILLIAM ARTHUR

Lesson 1

THE WORK OF
THE HOLY SPIRIT

What makes a Christian so different from anyone else? And even among Christians, why do some seem to have more winsomeness and power than others?

Merely to acknowledge the obvious differences in temperament, intelligence, and ability, as well as physical stamina, is not enough. Nor does pointing out the environmental and hereditary differences adequately answer the question. These are all factors which certainly influence personality, but they in themselves do not account for the basic differences in people.

The Divine Nature

Ultimately the decisive factor in human personality is not human at all. It is supernatural—the very Life of God released in Christ through the Holy Spirit. It is His power, His holiness, His love that makes your life different.

His work in you might be compared to electricity in a light bulb. There is no light in the glass, nor in the filament within the bulb. The light comes only when these materials receive the electric current for which the bulb was made. Similarly, there is no spiritual life or holiness in your natural state. It is the Spirit's power coming into you from God that makes your life fulfill its intended purpose.

Being a Christian is not just having the righteousness

of Christ imputed to you so that by faith you stand justified before God. If this were all there was to it, Christianity would be little more than a bookkeeping job in heaven. But the presence of the Holy Spirit assures you that the Christian life is much more than this. There is an actual impartation to you of the Divine Nature (2 Peter 1:4). You are literally made "a new creature: old things are passed away; behold, all things are become new" (2 Corinthians 5:17).

Think of what this means! The Eternal Spirit; the present Person of the Godhead, equal in glory with the Father and the Son; the very Being of truth and holiness— "dwelleth in you" (1 Corinthians 3:16). You are the "temple" in which He resides (1 Corinthians 6:19). God is in you. All your redeemed powers are at His command. Nothing could be more tragic in your Christian life than for this fact to be unknown or ignored.

God in Action

God is the Father in administration; God is the Son in revelation; but God is the Spirit in operation, so that wherever the power of God is manifest, you see the work of the Holy Spirit.

In the very beginning of time, it was by the Spirit that God created the worlds and set the stars in space. By the same mighty power, God still upholds that which He has made, and apart from the Spirit, the universe would revert to nothingness.

It was the Spirit Who made man a living soul and breathed into him the life of God. This original life of holiness was lost when the Spirit was withdrawn from man because of sin. Yet, in God's infinite love, the Holy Spirit always has sought to restore man to His fellowship. Every move that man makes back to God today testifies to this unceasing effort. Evangelism is altogether the work of the Holy Spirit.

It was the Spirit Who prepared the way for Christ's coming through the long centuries of the Old Testament. Not everyone felt His power, but those chosen people who did perform some significant service in God's unfolding redemptive purpose were qualified for the task by the Holy Spirit.

Finally, in the fullness of time, as you would expect, it was the Spirit Who planted the seed of God in the womb of the Virgin so that she conceived and brought forth the Holy Child. Thereafter, it was the Spirit Who led Jesus during the days of His incarnate ministry. All that He did in the flesh, He did in cooperation with the Spirit of God. He anointed Him to preach. He empowered Him to cast out demons. He sustained Him in suffering. At last, He enabled Him to offer up Himself to the Father as your sacrifice for sin, and then in death-rending triumph, He raised Him from the grave.

The Promise of the Comforter

From beginning to end, God's work is done in the power of the Holy Spirit. Yet this power is not some vague, impersonal energy in the universe. The Spirit is a Person in quality like Jesus, and the life He imparts to you by His indwelling is the Christ life.

This was given particular emphasis by Jesus in the last hours before He was taken to be crucified. He knew that His disciples could only carry on His work effectively as they experienced a deeper relationship with Himself through the Spirit. So following the Last Supper, He gathered His faithful ones around Him, and told them that He would send "Another Comforter" to take His place when He returned to the Father (John 14:16).

Jesus was not speaking here about an influence or a doctrine; He was speaking of One just like Himself Who would stand by His people—a real Person Who would fill

17

their lives with His own presence and power. Yet there was this difference. Whereas Jesus in the flesh was limited by His earthly body, now this physical barrier would be removed, and His disciples could abide always in His glorious fellowship.

Of course, the Spirit had already been at work in their lives, but in a more wonderful and enduring way, He was now to glorify Christ within them as a living reality. Until Christ had finished His work on earth, this possibility could not be fully realized. But when He returned to take His place at the right hand of the heavenly Throne, then it was that the Spirit of God was released in power upon His expectant church; not for a few years, but for an age; not on a few special individuals, but on all who would receive Him.

For this reason, your privileges today as a Christian are actually greater than those the disciples enjoyed with Jesus while they walked together along the dusty roads of Galilee. For to you, as to them at Pentecost, the Comforter has come. He is here now—Christ is present without any limitations to effect in you what He has already done for you, and of His power, there is no end.

FIND IT
FOR YOURSELF . . .

1. When did the Holy Spirit start to work on earth?
   Genesis 1:2 (Psalms 104:30)

   _____

2. How did the Spirit work through men in the Old Testament? Note the people mentioned in the following verses, and the work which they did in the Spirit:

   (1) Genesis 41:38, 39 _____

   (2) Exodus 31:2–5 _____

   (3) Numbers 11:16, 17 _____

   (4) Judges 6:34 _____

   (5) 1 Samuel 16:13 _____

   (6) What conclusion would you draw from this?

   _____

   _____

   _____

   _____

   _____

3. How does this relate to your view of the Scripture?
   1 Peter 1:10, 11; 2 Peter 1:21 (2 Timothy 3:16)

   _____

   _____

   _____

4. How was the Spirit instrumental in bringing God directly into the stream of human history?
   Matthew 1:18, 20 (Luke 1:35)

   _____

   _____

5. Having given the Son a human body, how did the Spirit continue to work in His incarnate life? Note the particular thing ascribed to the Spirit in:

   (1) Luke 4:1 _____

   (2) Luke 4:14 _____

   (3) Luke 4:18, 19 _____

   _____

   (4) Matthew 12:28 _____

6. What part did the Spirit play in the atonement finished by Christ on the cross? Hebrews 9:14

   _____

7. How did the Spirit work in the resurrection? Romans 8:11

   _____

8. What does the Holy Spirit always impart to those who receive Christ? John 6:63 (2 Corinthians 3:6)

_____

9. How close is the Spirit to every Christian? 1 Corinthians 3:16 (Romans 8:9)

_____

10. By virtue of the Spirit in you, what are some of your privileges through Christ?

(1) Ephesians 2:18 _____

(2) Jude 20 _____

(3) John 4:24 _____

(4) Romans 8:14 _____

11. Various fruits of the Spirit produced in your life are mentioned in Galatians 5:22, 23. Paraphrase each one in your own words.

_____

_____

_____

_____

_____

_____

12. What government exemplifies these spiritual virtues? Romans 14:17

_____

13. What obligation always rests upon those who live in this Kingdom? Galatians 5:16, 25 (1 John 2:6)

_____

_____

14. Note some concrete examples of the way the Spirit directed those that walked with Him in the early church. What was the occasion in the following instances:

(1) Acts 8:29 _____

_____

(2) Acts 10:19, 20 _____

_____

(3) Acts 13:2, 4 _____

_____

(4) Acts 15:22, 28 _____

_____

(5) Acts 16:6, 7 _____

_____

15. How does the Spirit react to disobedience? Ephesians 4:30

_____

16. The three chapters in John 14, 15, and 16 record the teaching of Jesus to His disciples on the eve of His death, and as such, comprise our greatest insight into the Person and work of the Holy Spirit. Read through this passage slowly, noting each reference to the Spirit, then answer the following questions:

(1) What is the Name given to the Holy Spirit most often in this passage?

_____

(2) Why would the Holy Spirit be such a Helper to the disciples? What significance does the use of the word "Another" have here? (14:16)

_____

_____

(3) What function does the Spirit have in relation to truth, and your understanding of it? (14:17, 26; 15:26; 16:13)

_____

(4) What is the supreme ministry of the Holy Spirit? (16:14)

_____

(5) Why cannot the unbelieving world receive the Holy Spirit? (14:16, 30; 15:21; 16:3, 8–11)

_____

_____

(6) Why do you think the privilege of prayer is emphasized so much in this passage? (14:13, 14; 15:7, 16; 16:23, 24, 26)

_____

_____

_____

17. In contrast to the way the Spirit moved upon selected individuals for special ministries in the Old Testament, who is included in the potential scope of the promised outpouring of the Holy Spirit in the church age? Joel 2:28 (Acts 2:17)

_____

18. What had to happen in relation to Jesus before the promise of the Comforter could be realized? John 7:39 (Acts 2:33)

_____

_____

_____

MAKE YOUR OWN APPLICATION . . .

Noting John 16:7, tell how Christ is more real to you since the Comforter has come. If you are not sure about it, then write what you think your experience should be as you understand the Scripture. Follow this same course where it applies in other questions throughout the book.

_____

_____

_____

_____

_____

_____

_____

_____

_____

Memorize . . . John 16:13, 14 and John 16:23

WORDS FOR REFLECTION . . .

The very fact that some of us believe one thing and some another does not do away with the fact that God says, "Be ye filled with the Holy Spirit." I believe this is the greatest need of the church of Jesus Christ today.

Everywhere I go I find that God's people lack something. God's people are hungry for something; God's people are thirsting for something. I find among professing Christians a great need and lack, a feeling of insecurity, and defeat in their Christian lives. . . .

The church today is powerless. We are gathering for our prayer meetings, church services, and Sunday school conventions. Committees meet; Bible classes are conducted; Bible schools are carried on, but we have no power because we do not have the Spirit of God in power and in fulness in our lives. The Bible says, "Be ye filled with the Spirit. . . . "

I want to say something very dangerous. Did you know that it is possible to work for the Lord and live an exemplary life without being filled with the Holy Spirit? It says concerning the Corinthians that they came behind in no gift (1 Corinthians 1:5–7). But Paul called them carnal Christians (1 Corinthians 3:1). This means that I can have the gift of an evangelist. I can get up and preach and still not be filled with the Spirit. I shall preach without power and my preaching will be as sounding brass and tinkling cymbal. You may have the gift of teaching a Sunday school class. You can have the gift without being filled with the Spirit. Because you can get up and talk or teach the Bible does not necessarily mean that you are filled with the Spirit. What an awful thing that is! . . .

I have asked God if there were ever a day when I should stand in the pulpit without knowing the fulness and anointing of the Spirit of God and should not preach with compassion and fire, I want God to take me home to heaven. I don't want to live. I don't ever want to stand in the pulpit and preach without the power of the Holy Spirit.

Some of you may have the gift of administration. You may have the gift of prophecy. You may have any of the other spiritual gifts mentioned in 1 Corinthians 12. You can have all of them and still not be filled with the Spirit! I ask you pastors, I ask myself, I ask you Sunday school teachers, you Christian workers, you church members—are you filled with the Holy Spirit?

BILLY GRAHAM

Quoted with permission from the sermon "How to Be Filled with the Spirit," in *Revival in Our Time* published by the Van Kampen Press.

Lesson 2

FILLED WITH THE SPIRIT

What happened to the disciples at Pentecost, and can it happen again?

That something unusual occurred there in the upper room is obvious. There was a "sound from heaven as of a rushing mighty wind. . . . And there appeared unto them cloven tongues like as of fire . . . " (Acts 2:2, 3). And what was even more startling to the crowds assembled in the city of Jerusalem on that day, the Christians went out on the streets and began to speak so joyfully "the wonderful works of God" in such diverse languages that the people thought they were drunk (Acts 2:5–13). Never had anything like that been seen before.

The Abiding Reality

However, the real power of Pentecost is not to be seen in these great manifestations of the Spirit's outpouring. They attested to God's Presence, but they were only temporary, and like the miraculous signs connected with the advent of the Son of God, need not be repeated.

The enduring miracle of Pentecost is not in the phenomena attending it, but rather in the reality of the experience of Christ which the waiting church received when they "were all filled with the Holy Spirit" (Acts 2:4). This was what made the difference, first in themselves, and then in the world where they lived their witness.

This experience marked a new era in the history of redemption. It was the culminating step in the descent of the divine into the human. Jesus as an external Presence now became the enthroned Sovereign in the hearts of His people. The Gospel became life and power within them, and the church of God went forth determinedly to fulfill the great commission.

The full significance of what this meant becomes increasingly apparent as one studies the Book of Acts. There was a new confidence and boldness in the witness of the disciples. Their hearts burned with the love of God. Attitudes of self-seeking among themselves were gone. They had much to learn, but their hearts were pure. In honor preferring one another, they sought first the Kingdom. Prayer became second nature. The Scriptures opened to them with new meaning and authority. Obedience was joyful. Nothing could defeat them—not the anger of mobs, nor the irritations of daily trials, nor beatings of tyrants, but as rivers borne along with loud rushing sound, they went on their way "with gladness and singleness of heart, praising God" (Acts 2:46, 47).

No wonder the world could not contain them. There was an aroma of heaven upon their lives. Christ was in their midst, and just as He had promised, they were doing the works which He had done (John 14:12). But more than His work, it was His Life filling their hearts with Himself that made the church so different and unconquerable.

The Norm of Christian Experience

It is this reality of being filled with the Spirit that gives to Pentecost an enduring quality. Again and again, mention is made in the Acts that this experience characterized the moving force of the church. In all kinds of situations, in life and in death, individually and collectively, specific reference is made to this spiritual condition undergirding the Christian community.

The words used to describe it are variable. Sometimes the emphasis is upon the act of being filled with the Spirit; at other times it is upon the state of acting in the spirit. But always the inspired Record underscores the fact, both as an event and as a life.

It accentuates the positive. Without becoming embroiled in theological speculation, the expression simply bears witness to a life situation—a life pervaded by the Spirit of our loving Saviour.

Needless to say, not everyone in the early church was filled with the Spirit. The accounts in the New Testament reflect some problems of strife and pettiness among the believers. However, where these conditions existed, the Spirit-filled reality, variously called, was urged upon the Christians as their privilege and obligation.

Your Privilege Today

This reality still holds good today. The problems which the early church faced were no less real than those which confront you, and God's provision to meet them no less sufficient. Nothing about the enduement of "power from on High" (Luke 24:49) has ever been outmoded. "The promise is unto you, and to your children, and to all that are afar off" (Acts 2:39).

As to that first Pentecost, some have said that the Spirit would have come whether the disciples had tarried or not. Be that as it may, only those who obeyed the Lord, and tarried, received the promise on that day.

So it is with the church today. It is not that a period of time must pass before the heart can be filled. It is simply that the heart must be ready. This is where the issue rests now. The Spirit will surely fill any vessel that is prepared. It remains for you to remove any barrier in His way.

31

Though your vessel may be small, still He can fill you to your capacity. After all, it is not that you get all of Him, but that He gets all of you.

Nor is it a once and for all thing. The command is to be filled with the Spirit continually, moment by moment (Ephesians 5:18). You need to look to God for a fresh outpouring of His Spirit each day. And from time to time, as new problems arise, doubtless you will feel the need for special anointings of the Spirit to meet the demands. So keep open to God; let no selfish rubbish clutter up your life; make Christ Lord in every situation, and you may be sure that the Spirit will continue to fill your soul with the "fulness of God" (Ephesians 3:19).

FIND IT
FOR YOURSELF . . .

1. What was the enduement of the Spirit especially to give the disciples? Luke 24:49 (Acts 1:8)

_____

2. How was it symbolized in the figure of baptism? Matthew 3:11 (Acts 1:5)

_____

3. The key to the Book of Acts, as well as its outline, is found in Acts 1:8. Write out a free translation of this verse in your own words.

_____

_____

_____

_____

_____

4. What were the disciples told to do in anticipation of the promise? Acts 1:4 (Luke 24:49)

_____

5. When was the promise realized? Acts 2:1–4, 16

_____

6. In addition to the 120 in the upper room at Pentecost, who else were specifically said to have been filled with the Spirit? Note those involved and the occasion in the following references:

   (1) Acts 4:8———————————————

   (2) Acts 4:31 ——————————————

   (3) Acts 6:3————————————————

   (4) Acts 6:5————————————————

   (5) Acts 7:55 ——————————————

   (6) Acts 9:17 ——————————————

   (7) Acts 11:24———————————————

   (8) Acts 13:9 ——————————————

   (9) Acts 13:52———————————————

7. What does the term "filled with the Spirit" mean to you?

   _____

   _____

8. In view of the fact that a number of people are involved in more than one reference to the infilling, what does this suggest to you about the repeated and abiding character of this experience?

   _____

   _____

9. The reception of the Holy Spirit by the believers at Samaria (Acts 8:5–17), Caesarea (Acts 10:1–48; 11:15–18; 15:7–9), and Ephesus (Acts 19:1–7), while not specifically said to be an infilling of the Spirit, is often associated with it. Review these passages, and summarize in a few words the greatest lesson you learn from these incidents.

_____

_____

_____

_____

10. What did the Holy Spirit do in the hearts of those who welcomed Him? Acts 15:9

_____

11. How did the Holy Spirit enable them to sing amid the trials and frustrations of their day? Acts 13:52 (Acts 2:46, 47)

_____

_____

12. In the face of opposition, what characterized their spoken witness? Acts 4:31; 14:3; 19:8

_____

_____

13. What did they talk about so naturally? Acts 5:42; 8:5; 9:20; 11:20

_____

_____

14. From what you know about the Holy Spirit, why would Christ be the focus of the Christian's witness?

_____

_____

15. An example of such a witness may be seen in Stephen, one of the first lay leaders of the church. Note:

   (1) In addition to being Spirit-filled, why was he selected for a church office? Acts 6:3, 5

   _____

   (2) What made his speech so powerful? Acts 6:10

   _____

   (3) What did he accuse the Jews of doing? Acts 7:51

   _____

   (4) How did the Spirit comfort him as he was being stoned to death? Acts 7:55, 56

   _____

   (5) What about his last thoughts reflected his deep experience of Christ? Acts 7:60

   _____

16. How did the Holy Spirit make the fellowship of the Christians together beautiful? Acts 2:44–47; 4:32–34

_____

_____

_____

17. What disciplines of the Holy life did the church practice together? Acts 2:42; 4:24–31; 12:12; 13:2, 3; 17:11

_____

_____

_____

_____

18. What demonstration of God's power frequently attended the witness of the church? Acts 2:43; 5:12; 6:8

_____

_____

_____

19. Whether there were physical miracles or not, what generally followed the Spirit-filled witness of the church? Acts 2:37, 47; 5:14; 6:7

_____

_____

_____

_____

20. As you have observed in reading the Acts, there was a great diversity of gifts and offices within the church. In this connection, read Romans 12:4–8, 1 Corinthians 12:4–31, and Ephesians 4:11–15, and note:

(1) Using the analogy of a body, why are there different gifts, and what purpose do they serve in the church?

_____

_____

_____

_____

_____

(2) Who determines which gift or gifts will be given and why? (12:11)

_____

_____

_____

_____

_____

21. What is the supreme result of the effective exercise of spiritual gifts? Ephesians 5:16 (1 Corinthians 13)

_____

_____

22. Irrespective of any particular gift which God may be pleased to give you, what is His continuing command? Ephesians 5:18

_____

_____

23. Immediately following this command, why do you think the Christians are told to praise God and to be subject one to another in the daily relationships of life, particularly within the home? Ephesians 5:19–6:9

_____

_____

MAKE YOUR OWN APPLICATION . .

State several ways in which you believe your family feels the effect of the Spirit's infilling in your life.

_____

_____

_____

_____

_____

_____

_____

_____

_____

_____

_____

_____

Memorize . . . Ephesians 5:18 and Acts 1:8

WORDS FOR REFLECTION . . .

Lord, I believe a rest remains
To all Thy people known,
A rest where pure enjoyment reigns,
And Thou art loved alone:

A rest where all our soul's desire
Is fixed on things above;
Where fear and sin and grief expire,
Cast out by perfect love.

O that I now the rest might know,
Believe and enter in!
Now, Saviour, now the power bestow,
And let me cease from sin.

Remove this hardness from my heart,
This unbelief remove:
To me the rest of faith impart,
The Sabbath of Thy love.

Come, Father, Son, and Holy Ghost,
And seal me Thine abode!
Let all I am in Thee be lost;
Let all be lost in God.

CHARLES WESLEY

Christian perfection does not imply (as some seem to have imagined) an exemption either from ignorance, or mistake, or infirmities, or temptations. Indeed, it is only another term for holiness. The essential part . . . is giving the heart wholly to God. Your present business is not to reason whether you should call your experience thus or thus, but to go straight to Him that loves you, with all your wants, how great or how many soever they are. Then all things are ready; help, when you ask, is given. You have only to receive it by simple faith. Nevertheless you will still be encompassed with numberless infirmities; for you live in a house of clay, and therefore this corruptible body will more or less press down the soul, yet not so as to prevent your rejoicing evermore and having a witness that your heart is all His. You may claim this: it is yours; for Christ is yours. Believe and feel Him near.

JOHN WESLEY

Lesson 3

THE PROBLEM OF SELF

What is the obstruction that prevents the Spirit from filling many Christians?

Certainly God does not want to withhold any good thing from His children. If there is a deficiency in this respect, then, it must be due to the unwillingness of the believer to let God have His way.

The Carnal Nature

This is the problem. All resistance to the will of God must be emptied out of you before the Spirit can fill you.

Sometimes this resistance may be difficult to identify, but it is known in the Bible as "carnality" or "the mind of the flesh" which is "enmity against God" (Romans 8:7). Actually this principle of evil is basically self-centeredness. Its symptoms may take many different forms, such as envy, pride, strife, bitterness, anger, bigotry, revengefulness, jealousy, touchiness, stinginess, pouting, fretting, or some other expression of inward hostility toward God. Wherever this condition is permitted to exist, the flow of the Spirit is clogged, and there is frustration and lack of power in your life.

Of course, if you are unaware of your selfish nature, as may be true of a young Christian living in the enthusiasm of a newfound joy, it may not bother your sense of peace and confidence in the Lord. This may explain why most Christians fail to see the need to do something about it until some bitter experiences have brought it to light.

When the first symptoms begin to come to your attention, probably you have no idea what the root of the matter is. All you know is that something is wrong, and like any good Christian, you confess your failure to God, promising to do better in the future. But as other evidences appear, more and more you become aware that in you "dwelleth no good thing" (Romans 7:18), and perhaps you are led almost to the point of despair, like Paul, when he cried out, "Who shall deliver me from the body of this death" (Romans 7:24)?

Then it is that this carnal disposition has to be faced for what it is. How you are able to deal with the problem, though, hinges on the way that you distinguish it from your essential human nature.

If, as many persons believe, it is so interwoven with your personality that it cannot be distinguished from humanity itself, then all you can do is tolerate it the rest of your life, or, at best, keep it under control. In this case, full relief can be expected only at death when at last your soul is released from your body, or as others claim, only after the fires of purgatory have purified the soul.

However, if you distinguish between your selfish attitude and the essential qualities of your human nature, you are in a position to deal decisively with the problem now. For humanity, like physical matter, is not evil in itself. It has become an instrument of sin, but basically the problem is not with your body, it is with your will—the stubborn, unyielded, independent self unwilling to let God have complete control over your life. For this reason, from this point of view, carnality as a perversion of the will can continue only by your lack of its perception or by your consent. That is why it does not need to be repressed, but crucified.

44

The Human Nature

On the other hand, no matter how dead you are to your carnal self, your human nature remains very much alive. If you fail to accept this fact and fail to interpret your present circumstances accordingly, your whole confidence in what God has done for you can be easily shaken.

In Christian experience your human qualities are not destroyed any more than your self-consciousness is destroyed. You are still a free man. As a free moral personality, you must constantly struggle against all the powers of darkness in this evil world. Temptation will always be real to you, and if you do not continue to yield yourself fully to the Spirit's control, the "old man" can rise again to defeat you.

What complicates the situation is that you must contend with the human limitations inherent in your body and mind. Regrettable as it is, you still have to live with ignorance, even though you try to improve your condition every way possible. Moreover, your physical body, despite all that you can do, is still going to get tired and sick. Then there are hereditary weaknesses which you have to accept. Sometimes, too, scars of the old life before you were converted can hinder your witness, notwithstanding God's forgiveness. Perhaps, also, there are some maladjustments in your behavior growing out of repressed complexes in childhood of which you are not aware. These, and many other involuntary traits, leave much to be desired in this life. Though you seek to overcome them, and can make progress through the help of God, the fact remains that you will not be delivered from most of these infirmities of the flesh until finally your body is glorified in the world to come.

The crucifixion of your carnal nature does not dehumanize you. It will permit the Spirit of Christ to gain the undisputed ascendancy of your will, but it does not deify your nature. You still have your problems, your sufferings, your sorrows. God can keep you sweet amid your trials; however, you will not be insensitive to annoyances or immune to the feelings of pain. You are still human.

Recognizing this truth, it is imperative that you maintain a strict discipline in your will, always keeping your body in subjection to your higher spiritual being. Indeed, in this sense, you must keep your humanity under control of the Spirit, repressing any tendency that might divert your allegiance from your Lord.

But you do not have to live with that rebellious spirit of carnality. It is sin, and through the blood of Jesus Christ, you can be cleansed from it by the Holy Spirit.

FIND IT
FOR YOURSELF . . .

1. What was the spiritual state of the disciples prior to their filling of the Spirit at Pentecost?

   (1) Luke 10:20 ————————————————

   (2) John 15:3 —————————————————

   (3) John 17:12 ————————————————

2. There can be little doubt that the obedient disciples of Jesus were saved before Pentecost, but still what unwholesome attitudes characterized their lives? Note the following: (It might be interesting to compare these traits with your own experience.)

   (1) Luke 9:52–55 ———————————————

   (2) Mark 9:34; 10:37 ————————————

   (3) Matthew 20:24 ————————————————

   (4) Mark 9:38, 39 —————————————————

   (5) Mark 10:13, 14 ———————————————

   (6) Mark 14:37–41————————————————

(7) John 18:18, 25 ——————————————

3. What did Jesus say that seemed so difficult for Peter to accept? Matthew 16:21–23 (Mark 8:31–33)

_____

_____

Why do you suppose this was the case?

_____

_____

4. What does Paul call this fleshly disposition that is at odds with God's will? Romans 8:7 (1 Corinthians 3:1, 4)

_____

5. How does this carnality, or fleshly nature, manifest itself in relation to spiritual things? Galatians 5:17 (Romans 8:5)

_____

6. Read the account of Paul's own struggle with carnality in Romans 7:7–25, noting expecially verse 18.

(1) What did he come to see about himself in the light of God's law?

_____

_____

(2) Why was there a conflict within him?

_____

_____

7. How is the carnal mind reflected in the church at Corinth? 1 Corinthians 3:1–4

_____

_____

8. What are some traits of the old nature which still seemed to trouble some of the saints at Ephesus? Ephesians 4:22–32 (Colossians 3:8–10)

_____

_____

_____

9. How does Paul get at the problem when writing to the Philippians? Philippians 2:3, 4, 14

_____

_____

10. What is the cause for instability in the Christian life according to James? James 1:8; 4:8

_____

_____

11. What attitude does God always resist? James 4:6 (1 Peter 5:5)

_____

12. What experience in the Old Testament illustrates the way people who have been saved by God can fail to enter into a victorious life of faith? Hebrews 3:15–19 (Numbers 14:26–33) Try to picture this in your mind.

_____

13. What finally is the crux of the problem with those who are defeated? Hebrews 3:12; 4:2

_____

14. How completely has God dealt with your sin in the atonement of Christ? Hebrews 9:26 (Colossians 2:14)

_____

15. How completely does God expect you to put away sin in your life? 2 Corinthians 7:1 (Hebrews 12:1)

_____

16. Read Romans 7:25–8:4, comparing several translations, and explain why full yieldedness to the Holy Spirit frees you from the old nature of sin and death.

_____

_____

_____

_____

_____

_____

17. Though free from the power of sin, what still remains to be disciplined in your life? 1 Corinthians 9:27

_____

_____

18. What other problem do you have to deal with? Ephesians 6:11, 12 (1 Peter 5:8, 9)

_____

_____

19. Study 2 Corinthians 10:3–5.

    (1) Why are your weapons against Satan so powerful?

    _____

    _____

    (2) What must you do with evil suggestions and imaginations when they arise out of your circumstances?

    _____

    _____

    _____

20. How was Jesus' temptation like yours? Hebrews 4:15 (Luke 4:2)

_____

_____

21. In addition to temptation, what are some of the problems which you experience that Jesus also endured in His perfect humanity?

    (1) Luke 2:40 ———————————————

    (2) Matthew 4:2 ———————————————

    (3) John 4:6 ————————————————

    (4) Matthew 26:38 ——————————————

22. What did Christ learn from His human suffering that is an example for you? Hebrews 5:8 (Philippians 2:8)

_____

_____

_____

23. What are some habits in Jesus' life which also teach you how to get help in strengthening your human nature?

(1) Luke 5:16 _____

(2) Luke 24:27 _____

(3) Luke 4:16 _____

24. How can your weaknesses in the body become to you a means of spiritual blessing? 2 Corinthians 12:9, 10

_____

_____

25. Who is present now to help you bear your infirmities of the body? Romans 8:26

_____

MAKE YOUR OWN APPLICATION . . .

Write out briefly how you recognized your need for a deeper cleansing of the Holy Spirit in your life.

_____

_____

_____

_____

_____

_____

_____

_____

_____

Memorize . . . Romans 8:1, 2 and James 4:6

WORDS FOR REFLECTION . . .

I awoke that morning hungering and thirsting just to live this life of fellowship with God, never again to sin. . . . Getting out of bed about six o'clock with that desire, I opened my Bible and, while reading some of the words of Jesus, He gave me such a blessing as I never dreamed a man could have this side of heaven. It was an unutterable revelation. It was a heaven of love that came into my heart. My soul melted like wax before fire. I sobbed and sobbed. I loathed myself that I had ever sinned against Him or doubted Him or lived for myself and not for His glory. Every ambition for self was now gone. The pure flame of love burned it like a blazing fire would burn a moth.

I walked out over Boston Commons before breakfast, weeping for joy and praising God. Oh, how I loved! In that hour I knew Jesus, and I loved Him till it seemed my heart would break with love. I was filled with love for all His creatures. I heard the little sparrows chattering; I loved them. I loved the dogs, I loved the horses, I loved the little urchins on the streets, I loved strangers who hurried past me, I loved the heathen—I loved the whole world.

I have never doubted this experience since. I have sometimes wondered whether I might not have lost it, but I have never doubted the experience any more than I could doubt that I had seen my mother, or looked at the sun. It is a living experience.

In time, God withdrew something of the tremendous emotional feelings. He taught me I had to live by my faith and not by my emotions. He showed me that I must learn to trust Him, to have confidence in His unfailing love and devotion, regardless of how I felt.

SAMUEL LOGAN BRENGLE

I tell you, as plain as I can speak, where and when I found this. I found it in the oracles of God, in the Old and New Testament; when I read them with no other view or desire but to save my soul. . . .

I say, again, let this perfection appear in its own shape, and who will fight against it? It must be disguised before it can be opposed.

This we confess (if we are fools therein, yet as fools bear with us) we do expect to love God with all our heart, and our neighbor as ourselves. Yea, we do believe, that He will in this world so "cleanse the thoughts of our hearts, by the inspiration of His Holy Spirit, that we shall perfectly love Him, and worthily magnify His holy Name."

JOHN WESLEY

Lesson 4

SIN AND PERFECTION

Can the Christian be made perfect in this life?

Sooner or later this question is sure to come up. It raises a very delicate problem, but it needs to be answered. Confusion at this point can cause you to live in defeat through constant condemnation of yourself just as it can lead, on the other extreme, to presumption and arrogance.

Holiness Required

Let it be settled in the beginning that God expects His people to be holy. He is "of purer eyes than to behold evil" (Habakkuk 1:13). Holy love is the essence of His nature. Without clean hands and a pure heart it is impossible to be accepted in His sight.

The whole purpose of Christ coming into the world was to make a way for man to be acceptable to God. To that end, He died "to redeem you from all iniquity" (Titus 2:14). "He appeared to put away sin by the sacrifice of Himself" (Hebrews 9:26). And by His grace, He saves "to the uttermost all that come unto God by Him" (Hebrews 7:25).

This is no academic matter. The blood of Jesus Christ opens to your believing heart an actual deliverance from sin whereby you are enabled by the Holy Spirit to "serve God without fear in holiness and righteousness . . . all the days of your life" (Luke 1:75).

Any time that you sin, then, it is in violation of your privileges as a Christian. You are free to do so, of course, but you can not get by with it. Deliberate sin will break the fellowship which you have with God, and your soul will come into condemnation. To live with the sense of Christ's Presence, your conscience must be void of offense.

Willful Transgression and Mistakes

As to how you understand a clear conscience, much depends upon your interpretation of sin. When sin is considered as any deviation from the absolute holiness of God, whether you are aware of it or not, then, of course, you must acknowledge that you sin unconsciously in "thought, word, and deed every day." To do otherwise would require that your mind has no marks of the depravity in the human race. According to this definition of sin, as far as your present experience of righteousness is concerned, you can think of yourself as being free of sin only in the sense of your standing before God by virtue of your identity in Christ.

On the other hand, when sin is considered as a transgression of the known will of God, it is possible to live in Christ each day with the knowledge that there is nothing between you and your Lord. In this case, a distinction is made between a sin of intent and a sin of ignorance or mistake. A sin of intent is a wrong choice issuing from an unholy motive. A mistake is a wrong choice issuing from a holy motive. This does not make the mistaken action any less short of God's Perfection, nor does it absolve you from the consequences resulting from it in this world, but it does mean that your heart is condemned only for what you willfully do against your God.

As an illustration, suppose that you were given permission to go hunting on a certain property, but as you went out to the farm, not knowing clearly the boundaries, you unknowingly crossed the property line. Actually you would be breaking the law by trespassing on another's land, and you might get arrested for it. Morally, however, you would like to think yourself innocent because you were not clearly aware of the boundaries. You made an honest mistake. But having been informed of your error, suppose you went out the next day, traversing the same trail, crossing the same boundary. Whether or not you got caught, you would be guilty of committing a deliberate transgression of the law. You would sin willfully.

Keeping this distinction in mind, there is no reason why your experience in Christ on this earth should not correspond with your standing in Him. Mistakes which you make because of your human imperfections will cause you much regret, and they must be corrected when the Spirit shows them to you, but errors in judgment can not condemn your soul when you do not know what they are.

Perfect Love

Sin, understood as willful transgression, can exist in you only as you permit it. God wants your full consent to His will, and when you choose His side against your own, you come out against sin. As far as you know your heart, you want to live completely set apart for your Lord.

If you do allow yourself to be overcome with temptation, and give way to sin, your heart is broken when you realize that you have given consent to something displeasing to God. In such an event, your normal recourse is to immediately ask Him to forgive you, and with a new resolve of faith, walk in the light of His holiness. But this gracious provision for restoration of His fellowship does not mean that you must continually sin. Rather, it underscores the need for constant holiness through the cleansing blood of Jesus, and emphasizes that if any sin does mar this abiding experience, then you should turn quickly to God in contrition. Thanks be unto God, you never have to go to bed at night with a guilty conscience.

The term "sinless perfection" probably confuses the

issue in the minds of many Christians for in any absolute sense, of course, only God is perfect. The only perfection which you can know is your total response to God's will as you know it in Christ. It is not a perfection in knowledge or in accomplishment; it is a perfection in love as God has given you the ability to love—the perfection of your desire to love God with all your heart, with all your soul, with all your mind, and to love your neighbor as yourself (Matthew 22:37-40). This is finally the summation of all the commandments of God.

Such love is holy because it is of God—His own Nature infused into your heart by the Holy Spirit. All you do is open your life fully to His control so that He can love Himself through you. Yet in this yieldedness, you know that your heart is free—free of anything known to be sin, free of condemnation, free of fear—all is well with your soul.

FIND IT
FOR YOURSELF . . .

1. What should your attitude always be toward sin? Psalms 97:10 (Proverbs 8:13)

   _____

   _____

2. Why is this your attitude? Psalms 99:9 (1 Peter 1:16)

   _____

3. Who alone can be acceptable in God's sight? Psalms 24:3–5 (Hebrews 12:14)

   _____

4. Study 1 Thessalonians 4:7, 8.

   (1) To what has God called you? _____

   _____

   (2) What does resistance to the call mean?

   _____

5. What was God's answer to the sin problem? Matthew 1:21 (Hebrews 7:25)

   _____

   _____

6. Write out Titus 2:14 in your own words.

_____

_____

_____

_____

7. How long does God expect you to live in holiness on this earth? Luke 1:75

_____

8. In line with this, what did Jesus tell those who received His blessing?

   (1) John 8:11 _____

   (2) John 5:14 _____

9. How did Paul counsel the Christians in regard to living in sin? 1 Corinthians 15:34 (Romans 6:12, 15)

_____

_____

10. Read carefully 1 John 3:1–10, noting especially what is said about sin. Use a modern translation, if possible.

    (1) How is sin defined? (3:4) _____

    _____

    (2) Why did Christ appear? (3:5, 8) _____

    _____

(3) How are Christians distinguished from others in the world? (3:1, 7, 10)

_____

_____

(4) Verses 6, 8, 9, and 10 speak of the contradiction of sin in the life of a Christian. The verbs here express a habitual action. They do not say that a Christian is incapable of commiting an act of sin, but they do clearly say that a Christian will not make a habit of sinning. With this in mind, write out in your own words a free translation of verse 9.

_____

_____

_____

_____

11. If you do sin, and fellowship with Christ is broken, what assurance do you have? 1 John 2:1

_____

_____

12. What danger is there to the man who keeps on sinning without regard to Christ, continually refusing to repent? Hebrews 10:26 (Again the verb in this verse expresses a habitual action.)

_____

_____

13. Where does Jesus locate the issue of sin? Mark 7:21–23 (Matthew 5:27, 28)

_____

14. Who alone is qualified to tell you specifically what sin is in your heart? Psalms 139:23, 24 (Jeremiah 17:10)

_____

15. As an example of how the measure of light may vary with Christians, note how the Spirit-filled Peter, like many others, lived for a long time with a wrong assumption.

(1) What was it? (Acts 10:28)

_____

(2) When God corrected his sincere though mistaken view, what did he do about it? (Acts 10:34)

_____

(3) Do you think there might be some practices now in your life conditioned by your training and surroundings which God will need to correct?——

16. Read the Sermon on the Mount in Matthew 5, 6, and 7, and then list several areas in your life where you feel there might be room for improvement. If you have any explicit idea what you can do about it, jot it down, too.

_____

_____

_____

_____

_____

_____

17. What is the standard for conduct which Jesus lays down for you? Matthew 5:48

_____

_____

18. Compare this with the great commandment of Jesus in Matthew 22:36–40. What strikes you as being at the heart of both, and explain why?

_____

_____

_____

_____

_____

19. What is the bond of perfectness? Colossians 3:14

_____

20. List the things which have no value apart from love as noted by Paul in 1 Corinthians 13:1–3.

_____

_____

_____

21. Picture in your way of speaking the marks of love described in 1 Corinthians 13:4–7.

_____

_____

_____

_____

_____

_____

_____

_____

_____

22. Where does such love come from? Romans 5:5 (1 John 4:7)

_____

23. Why does perfect love give you confidence and peace? 1 John 4:18

_____

_____

66

MAKE YOUR
OWN APPLICATION . . .

Noting Paul's testimony in Acts 23:1 and 24:16, tell how your conscience backs up your witness of heart purity. Refer also to 1 Timothy 1:5 and 1 John 3:21.

_____

_____

_____

_____

_____

_____

_____

_____

_____

_____

_____

Memorize . . . Mark 12:30, 31 and 1 John 4:16

WORDS FOR REFLECTION . . .

I felt the ingratitude, the danger, the sin of not living nearer to God. I prayed, agonized, fasted, strove, made resolutions, read the Word more diligently, sought more time for meditations—but all without avail. . . . Each day brought its register of sin and failure, of lack of power. To will was indeed "present with me," but to perform I found not.

Then came the question, is there no rescue? Must it be thus to the end—constant conflict, and too often defeat? I felt I was a child of God. His Spirit in my heart would cry, in spite of all, "Abba, Father." But to rise to my privileges as a child, I was utterly powerless.

All the time I felt assured that there was in Christ all I needed, but the practical question was—how to get it out. I strove for faith, but it would not come; I tried to exercise it, but in vain. Seeing more and more the wondrous supply of grace laid up in Jesus, the fulness of our precious Saviour, my guilt and helplessness seemed to increase.

When my agony of soul was at its height, a sentence in a letter from dear McCarthy was used to remove the scales from my eyes, and the Spirit of God revealed to me the truth of our oneness with Jesus as I had never known it before. He wrote: "But how to get faith strengthened? Not by striving after faith, but by resting on the Faithful One."

As I read, I saw it all! "If we believe not, He abideth faithful." I looked to Jesus and saw (and when I saw, oh, how joy flowed!) that He had said, "I will never leave thee."

"Ah, there is rest!" I thought. "I have striven in vain to rest in Him. I'll strive no more."

I saw not only that Jesus will never leave me, but that I am a member of His body, of His flesh and of His bones. . . . The sweetest part, if one may speak of one part being sweeter than another, is the rest which full identification with Christ brings. I am no longer anxious about anything, as I realize this; for He, I know, is able to carry out His will, and His will is mine. It makes no difference where He places me, or how. That is rather for Him to consider than for me; for in the easiest position He must give His grace, and in the most difficult His grace is sufficient.

Nor should we look upon this experience, these truths, as for the few. They are the birthright of every child of God, and no one can dispense with them without dishonoring our Lord. The only power for deliverance for sin or for true service is Christ.

HUDSON TAYLOR

Lesson 5

CONDITIONS TO BE MET

How does one become Spirit-filled? What is the secret of constantly abiding in Christ?

Continuing Obedience

To say that it is perfect love underscores the ethical quality of the condition, but from a practical point of view, love is expressed by obedience, which is the evidence of faith.

God gives the Holy Spirit "to them that obey Him" (Acts 5:32). Your soul is purified "in obeying the truth through the Spirit unto unfeigned love of the brethren" (1 Peter 1:22). The blood of Jesus Christ continues to cleanse from all sin as you "walk in the light as He is in the light" (1 John 1:7). When this fundamental condition for fellowship with Christ is followed, you should be victorious each step of the way to heaven. Full obedience is perfect happiness when you have unquestioned confidence in Him Whom you obey.

But it is a continuous walk. God never leaves your soul idle and without growth in His Perfection. No sooner will you respond to truth in one area of your life than light will be given in some new direction. For this reason, it is inevitable that along the journey you come to see the inner conflict of self-love, and begin to long for that promised rest.

This desire for something better does not go unrewarded. God "satisfies the longing soul" (Psalms 107:9). Those that hunger and thirst after righteousness shall be filled (Matthew 5:6). Mark it down! When you want God's best more than anything else, you will always find it.

Confession of Sin

Obedience, of course, brings you to confess any sin when it is pointed out by the Spirit. This means simply that you acknowledge that what God says about your condition is true. When you confess sin, you do not try to hide it, ignore it, or explain it away. But with a broken and contrite heart, you admit the specific transgression committed, asking forgiveness of any person or persons concerned directly in the offense, and offering to make appropriate amends.

Usually the closer you get to the root of your problem of carnality, the harder it gets to face it. But face yourself you must, confessing your deceitful ego to God, and as with anything else know to be contrary to His holiness, asking Him to cleanse you from it.

Full Consecration

There must also be a complete yielding of yourself to God. Your commitment to Christ begun at conversion thus takes on a deeper significance when egotism is nailed to the cross. In a way not known before, you reckon yourself "to be dead unto sin" (Romans 6:11) and "crucified with Christ" (Galatians 2:20). Renouncing your right to yourself, "as a living sacrifice" (Romans 12:1), you abandon all that you are to Jesus.

Whatever it might cost is accepted in advance. It is as though you write your name on a blank check and ask God to fill in the amount which He pleases. You have no desire to be freed from His service, regardless of any suffering and hardship it might entail, even if God would take the sweetness of His Presence from you. You count yourself as nothing but clay in the Potter's Hand.

Such consecration is a fundamental law of the abundant life. Except a grain of wheat fall to the earth and die, it can not bring forth fruit (John 12:24). If there is any resistance to this condition, or if you think yourself better than others because of your compliance with it, then you have not yet fathomed the depths of the carnal mind. In the light of God's love for you, and His sacrifice at Calvary, full and unconditional surrender is your only reasonable response.

Faith

Yet, it is not anything that you do that gives the victory. Confession and consecration only prepare your heart to receive the grace of God. The victorious life comes when you actually trust yourself into the possession of Him Who gave Himself for you. Giving up all to Him, you quit your striving, and start resting, just as you would leave an offering upon an altar.

In the final analysis, the infilling of the Spirit, like any other benefit of salvation, is a gift of God. You do not have to beg God for it. The Gift is already present. Indeed, He is in you. All you have to do is to believe that He possesses your empty vessel. You know that the Father delights to "give the Holy Spirit to them that ask Him" (Luke 11:13), and if you "ask anything according to His will," you know that He will grant your petition (1 John 5:14, 15).

Your sanctification, then, ultimately rests upon your faith in the Word of God (John 17:17)—the faith that God has chosen you in Christ "before the foundation of the world" that you should be "holy and without blame before him in love" (Ephesians 1:4); the faith that Christ "loved the church and gave Himself for it, that He might sanctify and cleanse it" (Ephesians 5:26); the faith that His precious blood appears in the Holy Place to "purge your conscience from dead works to serve the living God" (Hebrews 9:14); the faith that "where sin abounded, grace did much more abound" (Romans 5:20); the faith that God "is able to do exceedingly abundantly above all that we ask or think, according to the power that worketh in" you (Ephesians 3:20); the faith that the Spirit and the Bride bid you come and drink freely from the living waters (Revelation 22:17).

These and a thousand other promises in the Book testify that God is for you, and that all the resources of heaven are available for your full salvation. When you take Him at His Word, not relying on felt impressions or gifts, but believing only that He shall do what He says, then you may confidently rest in His faithfulness, "for He is faithful that promised" (Hebrews 10:23).

After all, it is not who you are, but Who He is that makes the difference. Rejoice in it. "Faithful is He that calleth you, Who also will do it" (1 Thessalonians 5:24).

FIND IT
FOR YOURSELF . . .

1. What does Jesus promise to you in return for your love? John 14:21, 23

2. How is this abiding fellowship maintained and perfected? 1 John 2:5, 6 (John 15:10)

3. What does God give to you through obedience? Acts 5:32

4. What does obedience indicate? Hebrews 11:7, 8 (Genesis 6:9; 17:2)

5. Note Jesus' teaching in John 8:31, 32.

    (1) Who are the disciples of Jesus?

    (2) What do you come to know in this relationship?

(3) What does this knowledge do?

_____

6. Paraphrase in your own words 1 John 1:7.

_____

_____

_____

_____

7. What desire does God honor in satisfying your soul?
   Psalms 107:9 (Matthew 5:6)

_____

8. What quality of life characterizes those who receive
   more grace? James 4:6 (1 Peter 5:5)

_____

9. When sin is known in your life, what must you do
   about it in order to maintain fellowship with your
   Lord? 1 John 1:9 (Proverbs 28:13)

_____

10. Read the prayer of penitence in Psalms 51, and sum-
    marize in a sentence what it teaches you about genuine
    confession in regard to:

    (1) Honesty————————————————————

    _____

    (2) Brokenness ————————————————————

    _____

(3) Obedience ————————————————

————————————————————————————————

(4) Cleansing ————————————————

————————————————————————————————

11. If fellowship is broken with other people, who is responsible for taking the initiative in seeking to restore confidence? Matthew 18:15; 5:24

————————————————————————————————

12. Read the account of the meeting of the disciples in the upper room before Pentecost in Acts 1:12–2:1, and note what you find in regard to:

(1) Prayer ——————————————————

————————————————————————————————

(2) Study of the Scripture————————————

————————————————————————————————

(3) Fellowship together ————————————

————————————————————————————————

13. What three things did Jesus say that those who follow Him must do? Matthew 16:24 (Luke 9:23)

(1) ————————————————————————

(2) ————————————————————————

(3) ————————————————————————

14. Think about the paradox in the way this teaching is accepted. Matthew 16:25 (Luke 9:24)

    (1) To try to save life is to ─────────────

    (2) To lose your life for Christ is to ─────────

    (3) Why would you say this is the case?

    ────────────────────────────────

    ────────────────────────────────

    ────────────────────────────────

    ────────────────────────────────

15. Using an analogy of nature, what did Jesus teach as the fundamental requirement for fruitfulness? John 12:24, 25

    ────────────────────────────────

16. Then how must you reckon yourself in regard to sin? Romans 6:11 (1 Peter 2:24)

    ────────────────────────────────

17. What does Galatians 5:24 mean to you?

    ────────────────────────────────

    ────────────────────────────────

    ────────────────────────────────

    ────────────────────────────────

18. How did Paul look upon his own achievements? Philippians 3:7, 8

_____

_____

19. Study carefully Paul's testimony in Galatians 2:20. Try to put yourself in his place.

   (1) How are you associated with Christ? ———

   _____

   (2) Yet what is the paradox? ———

   _____

   (3) How do you live in Christ ———

   _____

   (4) Why is such dedication reasonable?

   _____

   _____

   _____

20. When you get right down to it, what actually brings sanctification to you? Acts 26:18; 15:9

_____

21. Using the analogy of a gift laid on the altar, why do you believe that your dedication is accepted by God, and therefore made holy? Exodus 29:37; Matthew 23:19

_____

_____

22. Read Hebrews 10:19–23, and note:

(1) Why do you have boldness to ask God for cleansing? (10:19–21)

_____

_____

(2) How must you draw near to God? (10:22)

_____

_____

(3) What about the nature of God gives you confidence? (10:23)

_____

_____

23. Why do you know that God is pleased to give the Spirit when you ask Him? 1 John 5:14, 15; Luke 11:13

_____

_____

_____

_____

24. Sum up Luke 11:13 in terms of your request.

_____

_____

_____

MAKE YOUR OWN APPLICATION . . .

Review your answers in this lesson, and then tell how you have responded to the conditions for the Spirit's fullness.

_____

_____

_____

_____

_____

_____

_____

_____

Memorize . . . 1 Peter 1:22 and Galatians 2:20

WORDS FOR REFLECTION . . .

At my entrance into religion, I took a resolution to give myself up to God, as the best return I could make for His love, and, for the love of Him, to renounce all besides. . . . Such was my beginning, and yet I must tell you that for the first ten years I suffered much. The apprehension that I was not devoted to God as I wished to be, my past sins always present to my mind, and the great unmerited favors which God did me, were the matter and source of my sufferings. During this time I fell often, and rose presently.

When I thought of nothing but to end my days in these troubles (which did not at all diminish the trust I had in God, and which served only to increase my faith), I found myself changed all at once; and my soul, which till that time was in trouble, felt a profound inward peace, as if she were in the center and place of rest.

Ever since that time I walk before God simply, in faith, with humility and with love, and I apply myself diligently to do nothing and think nothing which may displease Him. . . . As to what passes in me at present, I cannot express it. I have no pain or difficulty about my state, because I have no will but that of God, which I endeavor to accomplish in all things, and to which I am so resigned that I would not take up a straw from the ground against His order, or from any motive than purely that of love to Him . . . . And I make it my business only to persevere in His holy presence, wherein I keep myself by simple attention, and a general fond regard to God, which I may call actual presence of God. . . .

As for set hours of prayer, they are only a continuation of the same exercise. Sometimes I consider myself there as a stone before a Carver, whereof He is to make a statue; presenting myself thus before God, I desire Him to form His perfect image in my soul, and make me entirely like Himself. . . .

The time of business does not differ from the time of prayer, and in the noise and clatter of my kitchen, while several persons are at the same time calling for different things, I possess God in as great tranquility as if I were upon my knees at the blessed sacrament. . . .

We must, nevertheless, always work at it, because not to advance in the spiritual life is to go back. . . . Let all our employment be to know God; the more one knows Him, the more one desires to know Him. And as knowledge is commonly the measure of love, the deeper and more extensive our knowledge shall be, the greater will be our love.

BROTHER LAWRENCE

Lesson 6

CRISIS AND PROCESS IN SANCTIFICATION

When does sanctification begin? Is it a process or an event? Can it be complete in this life?

The issue raised in these questions is often a matter of contention, and it occurs primarily because sanctification is not kept in Scriptural balance.

A Divine Process

Basically the word "sanctify" means, in its sacred use, to set apart for God or to make holy, and therefore it takes on the meaning of separation. The noun "saint" is applied to persons who have been sanctified. "Holiness" comes from the same word, and refers to the nature of that which belongs to God.

A problem inevitably arises when sanctification is made to refer almost exclusively to the cleansing of the carnal nature of man following conversion. That sanctification embraces this experience is true, but it has a much wider meaning.

Actually the whole work of the Holy Spirit in conforming the believer to the image of Christ falls within the sphere of sanctification. As such, it begins at conversion when you are "born of the Spirit" (John 3:8). Thus, it can be said that "if any man have not the Spirit of Christ, he is none of His" (Romans 8:9). Every Christian, in this sense, is sanctified, and may be called properly a saint.

However, this is only the beginning. The sanctifying Spirit will never stop trying to bring every area of your life "unto the perfect man, unto the measure of the stature of the fulness of Christ" (Ephesians 4:13). Sanctification thereby becomes a process throughout life by which the obedient child of God progressively is changed into the likeness of Christ, "from glory to glory, even as by the Spirit of the Lord" (2 Corinthians 3:18).

Entire Sanctification

What is sometimes called "entire sanctification," or as Luther translated this compound word in 1 Thessalonians 5:23, sanctification "through and through," is an expression that points to a particular work of the Spirit in the developing process of redemption. It is never intended to suggest that this is where sanctification begins or ends. While it involves a definite confrontation of truth in relation to the self life, nonetheless, it is only a part of the continuing sanctifying process.

Because the nature of this particular point in Christian experience requires the deepest commitment of the will, the decision which it forces often stands out as a monumental crisis. The carnal self does not die easily, and for those who struggle against the claims of God, the final agony of the struggling ego might resemble the last gasps of a puffed-up pillowcase before it goes through an old washing machine wringer. In such cases, when the last yes to the will of God is finally wrung out, it is not unusual for the soul to feel such a release that there is scarcely room to contain the erupting joy. With others there may be no struggle at all, and the crisis of decision may come so gradually, almost without feeling and interwoven with so many other things, that knowledge of its reality may be only the quiet awareness that it has come.

The manner and form will vary in each case, and it is dangerous to try to force it into any prescribed pattern. God made each person different. He suits the blessing to you as He knows best. Whether or not it is accompanied by some dramatic sign or intense emotional feeling at a particular point in time makes the fact of the cleansing and infilling no less real.

It is this definiteness about the fact of the experience itself which prompts some people to speak of it as "a second work of grace." The expression is not meant to depreciate the first work, but rather to say that when the Christian comes to see the conflict caused by this selfish nature, and is willing to surrender the problem to God, that the sanctifying grace received at the beginning is also adequate to meet this deeper need.

Continuing Growth

There will be many other crises in your life growing out of your developing experience of Christ's obedience. Some of these problems will present to you very real spiritual battles, and doubtless will stand out as epochal events in your Christian growth. In facing these decisions, however, you should have the inward strength of a heart already fully committed to the will of God.

Yet, this is a commitment that must be renewed in some way each time a decision of any kind is made, for everything that comes up—in the family, at school, on the job—involves your dedication to Christ. For this reason, it would be better not to think of full consecration primarily as a crisis, but as a life. The life is made up of a constant series of decisions, and how you make each one will determine the blessedness of your experience in following Christ.

As has been intimated several times, full yieldedness to the Spirit does not imply that you are completely mature in Christ. The "second blessing," if it may be called that, merely prepares the way for greater blessings, and growth in the image of Christ is accelerated. Death to self has implications in devotion and service of which you have now no comprehension, but God will be faithful to reveal them to you in the days ahead as you are able to bear them.

So rejoice that there is no foreclosure on progress. No matter what you have experienced thus far, the best is yet to be. As your knowledge of God's purpose grows, and your corresponding obedience of faith enlarges to embrace it, there will be a continual expanding of the Spirit's fullness in your life, even as your days of grace lengthen into the timeless dimensions of eternity.

Your goal is nothing less than the very Perfection of Jesus Christ. While it remains ever a vision beyond your experience, it is nevertheless a constant incentive to keep pressing on to higher ground, reaching always "toward the mark for the prize of the high calling of God in Christ Jesus" (Philippians 3:14). The closer you get to the heavenly city, the more your soul will long to see His face. Though it does not yet appear what you shall be, you know that when He does appear, you shall be "like Him," for you "shall see Him as He is" (1 John 3:2).

FIND IT
FOR YOURSELF . . .

1. How is God's plan of salvation being realized in your life? 2 Thessalonians 2:13 (1 Peter 1:2)

_____

_____

2. Who are the saints? 1 Corinthians 1:2 (Ephesians 1:1)

_____

_____

3. Note in 2 Corinthians 3:18:

   (1) Into Whose image are you being changed?

   _____

   (2) Who changes you? _____

   (3) When are you changed? _____

   (4) Why do you see Christ now as in a glass?

   _____

4. Write 1 Corinthians 13:12 in your own words. Compare your statement with a modern translation.

_____

_____

5. When will you see Jesus face to face? 1 John 3:2 (Revelation 22:4)

_____

6. How do you expect to be presented to Christ when He comes again? Jude 24 (Revelation 14:5)

_____

7. How does the anticipation of your future life affect your living now? 1 John 3:3 (2 Peter 3:14)

_____

_____

8. Sum up your present situation in the thought of Philippians 2:15.

_____

_____

9. What must you do with your selfish nature when it is recognized? Ephesians 4:22; Romans 6:12, 13, 19

_____

_____

10. The verbs in the above verses indicate a completed action. What does this mean in terms of your commitment?

_____

_____

11. Study 1 Thessalonians 5:23, 24, and note:

    (1) To what extent is sanctification possible?

    _____

    (2) What part of your personality can be preserved blameless?

    _____

    _____

    (3) Why can you believe God to do this?

    _____

    _____

    (4) When is this to happen?

    _____

12. Note the presentation called for in Romans 12:1. In what sense does this decision bring you to a crisis?

_____

_____

_____

13. There is a definite act of consecration to God, but in what sense is there also a continuing decision of self-denial? Romans 12:2

_____

_____

_____

14. Renewing your dedication continually, in what do you increase day by day as God gives you more grace?

   (1) Colossians 1:10————————————

   _____

   (2) 1 Thessalonians 3:12 ————————

   _____

   (3) 2 Corinthians 9:10 ————————

   _____

   (4) Colossians 2:19————————————

   _____

15. What is the goal in your Christian growth? Colossians 1:28 (Ephesians 4:15)

   _____

   _____

16. What is especially a problem with immaturity? Ephesians 4:14

   _____

   _____

   _____

17. Give a definition of a full-grown man according to Ephesians 4:13.

   _____

   _____

   _____

   _____

18. Note in Philippians 3:12–15:

    (1) What is his objective? ————————
    _____

    (2) What is he doing about it?————————
    _____

    (3) Though Paul says he has not attained perfectly his
        goal, yet in what sense is he perfect? ————
    _____

    _____

    (4) What about the imperfections in his life?
    _____

    _____

    _____

19. As you press on, like Paul, what must you always keep
    before you? Acts 26:19 (Colossians 3:1, 2)

    _____

    _____

    _____

20. In terms of your character, how do you see yourself in
    heaven? Revelation 19:8; 21:27; 22:4

    _____

    _____

    _____

MAKE YOUR OWN APPLICATION . . .

Read 1 Peter 2:21–24 and Philippians 2:5–8. As you think upon the example which Christ has given you, what are some things about His perfect life which challenge you to be more like your Master? Make these aspirations into resolutions, and then write out the three which have the greatest priority in your thinking now.

_____

_____

_____

_____

_____

_____

_____

Memorize . . . Romans 12:1,2 and Colossians 1:28

WORDS FOR REFLECTION . . .

O my God! Thou alone canst give the peace which we experience in this state. The more the soul offers itself freely and without falling back upon itself, the more it is at liberty. So long as it does not hesitate to lose all and to forget itself, it possesses all.

O Bridegroom of souls, Thou lettest the souls which do not resist Thee experience in this life an advance taste of that felicity. We want nothing and we want all. As it is only the creature which bounds the heart, the heart, never being contracted by the attachments to creatures nor by conversion to self, enters so to speak into Thine immensity. Nothing stops it. It loses itself more and more in Thee. But although its capacity grows infinitely, Thou dost entirely fill it. It is always brimming over.

That, my God, is the true and pure worship in spirit and in truth. Thou seekest such worshippers, but Thou dost scarcely find them. Nearly all seek themselves in Thy gifts, instead of seeking Thee alone by the cross and by deprivation. We want to guide Thee, instead of letting ourselves be guided by Thee. We give ourselves to Thee to become great, but we hold back since we have to let ourselves be made small. We say that we cling to nothing, and we are frightened by the slightest loss. We want to possess Thee, but we do not want to lose ourselves so that we can be possessed by Thee. This is not loving Thee. This is wanting to be loved by Thee. O God!

The creature does not realize why Thou hast made it. Teach it and impress in the depths of its heart that the clay should allow itself unresistantly to take all the shapes that the Potter pleases.

FRANCOIS FENELON*

Fear not to take the irrevocable step, and to say that thou hast once and for all given up self to the death for which it has been crucified in Christ. And trust Jesus the crucified One to hold self to the cross, and to fill its place in thee with His own blessed resurrection life. . . . In the restfulness and peace and grace of the new life thou shalt have unceasing joy at the wondrous exchange that has been made—the coming out of self to abide in Christ alone.

ANDREW MURRAY

---

*Used with permission from Harper and Row's edition of Fenelon's *Christian Perfection*, edited by Charles F. Whitson and translated by Mildred Whitney Stillman.

Lesson 7

THE CHRISTLIKE LIFE

What finally is the expression of your self-emptied, Spirit-filled life? How does the Holy Spirit manifest Himself through you?

Partaking of His Life

This question is not difficult to answer, although it will take eternity to disclose its meaning. For when all is said and done, holiness, being the nature of God, is nothing more nor less than Christlikeness.

It is the Christ life which the Spirit imparts to you. The holiness which you possess is only by virtue of your participation in His nature. Never forget it! Christ is the Holy One, and all you do is let Him live His life through you. Though your capacity to experience His fullness will grow as you mature in grace, at least when you are full of His Spirit, you know that He has all that there is of you at the moment. He is Lord of all.

You love Him supremely, not for what He has given you, but for His own sake. His pleasure is your happiness. Nothing gives you more delight than contemplating His holiness and glory. All you want is more grace to be like Him.

As long as you abide in this disposition, you have perfect peace. Discouragement and anxiety, to the extent that they spring from selfishness, are gone. The conflict of interest is settled. Christ has conquered every enemy, so what have you to fear? And since your reputation and ambition are crucified with Him, what have you to lose? Whatever He chooses for you is accepted joyfully. Whether you live, you live unto the Lord. Whether you die, you die unto the Lord. Whether you live or die, therefore, you are the Lord's (Romans 14:8).

In His abiding, there can be no defeat, for His life is your life; His death is your death; His resurrection is your resurrection; His ascension is your ascension, and His victory is your victory.

Personal Integrity and Discipline

In practical ethics, His likeness is most obvious in the transparent sincerity and integrity of your life. There is no sham about it. Nothing phony. Be it at church, in the home, at work or play, you are the same. Men may not appreciate some of your peculiar traits, and probably with good reason, but they should know that your word is true and your character beyond reproach. Nothing so discounts the witness of holiness as inconsistency in ethical behavior.

You must call yourself to strict account. People look to you as the representative of Jesus Christ, as indeed you are, and any blemish on your name is a reflection upon what men will think of His. So protect His honor jealously. "Abstain from all appearance of evil" (1 Thessalonians 5:22). Whenever the Spirit checks you in the least degree, make things right without delay. Mistakes which are made may be observed by others, but let them also see the readiness with which you make apology and earnestly seek through correction to become more like the Master.

The sincerity of your desire to grow in His image is evidenced by your personal devotional life. Carelessness at this point will undermine your highest aspirations. With this in mind, let nothing keep you from communion with God every day through the Word and prayer. Protect your quiet times. Listen to the Spirit of Christ within you. Cultivate the practice of the presence of God in the simple, common, routine chores of living. Here is the index of your spiritual vitality.

Serving Others

Your devotion to God in turn overflows in loving service to those whom He loves and whom Christ died to save. It is in this area where your sanctification finds its deepest relevance to the world. No longer preoccupied with your own frustrations, but motivated by Calvary love, you enter wholeheartedly into the redemptive ministry of your Lord.

In this respect, Jesus sanctified Himself. Not that He needed cleansing or empowering, but that He willingly and continually gave Himself to those He loved that they "might be sanctified through the truth" (John 17:19).

If this dimension of sanctification is neglected, your cleansing from sin and empowering for victorious living would seem to revolve around a selfish purpose, and thereby, repudiate the very thing from which you are delivered. The Spirit's work within your heart cannot be self-contained. His sanctification results in making you "a vessel unto honor," not to gratify your desire for personal blessing, but to make you "meet for the Master's use, prepared unto every good work" (2 Timothy 2:21). As Jesus said, "After that the Holy Spirit is come upon you, you shall be witnesses unto Me," beginning where you are, and reaching out to the ends of the earth (*see* Acts 1:8).

You dare not be insensitive to the needs of others, for you are a minister of Christ, feeling His compassion, bearing His suffering, "being made conformable unto His death" (Philippians 3:10). Even as He has given you the example, now by His Spirit you must "follow in His steps" (1 Peter 2:21).

It will not be easy. There will be many trials. Men will sometimes misunderstand you, and perhaps even revile you. You may see many failures. Those whom you seek to help may not always appreciate your labors. But that is not your concern; it is God's affair. It is your part only to trust and obey. Stay sweet. Keep singing. Return good for evil. Rejoice in your adversities, for in so doing, you show the praise of Him Who has called you out of darkness into light.

Remember that you never stand alone. Your ministry is shared by the whole body of Christ, the church. As your vision of His mission grows, so also will your sense of need and appreciation for the fellowship of the blood-washed saints of God. Your love for one another actually becomes to the world an illustration of Christ's love. So make it what it should be. Carry one another's burdens. Work together in the bonds of Him Who is Head of the body, that you may be one in Christ, and "that the world may believe" on Him whom the Father has sent (John 17:21).

FIND IT
FOR YOURSELF . . .

1. What could the world see in the lives of the unlearned yet Spirit-filled disciples of the early church? Acts 4:13

_____

2. How was Christ normally called by the church? Acts 10:36 (Romans 14:9)

_____

3. What does it mean to say that Christ is Lord of all? Romans 14:8 (2 Corinthians 5:15)

_____

_____

_____

4. Read the prayer of Paul for the church in Ephesians 3:14–21.

   (1) Summarize in a few words what he wants the Christians to know. (3:17–19)

   _____

   _____

   _____

   _____

(2) How is this to be realized? (3:16, 20)

_____

5. Write the formula for a victorious life as found in Romans 13:14.

_____

_____

_____

6. How does this affect the way that you go about your daily work? Colossians 3:23, 24 (2 Corinthians 5:9)

_____

_____

7. Read the 12th chapter of Romans, noting particularly the various duties of the Christian which are spelled out in verses 6–21. Write down a few of the qualities mentioned which you feel need more attention in your life.

_____

_____

_____

_____

_____

8. Why do the things which you suffer for Christ's sake help you? 2 Corinthians 1:5, 6 (Colossians 1:24)

_____

_____

_____

9. What does God's chastening do for you?
   Hebrews 12:5–11

   _____

   _____

   _____

10. What is the practical purpose of sanctification? 2 Timothy 2:21 (1 Peter 1:22)

   _____

   _____

11. From what you know about the Holy Spirit, why would you naturally expect sanctification to have an outgoing application? In this connection, look at John 7:38 and Hebrews 13:12, 13.

   _____

   _____

12. What is the measure of your love to others? John 13:34 (1 John 3:16)

   _____

   _____

13. How do you manifest your love to Christ?
    John 21:15–17 (Matthew 25:35–40)

   _____

   _____

   _____

14. Observe in Matthew 9:35–38 the way Jesus ministered to the people:

(1) How was He moved when He saw the multitudes? (9:36)

_____

(2) Why did He feel sorry for the people? (9:36)

_____

_____

(3) What was the need of the hour? (9:37, 38)

_____

_____

(4) List five people who are potential laborers in the harvest that you will remember in prayer.

_____

_____

_____

_____

15. One of the greatest chapters in the Bible is the High Priestly Prayer Of Jesus in John 17. Read it slowly, then go back and note:

(1) What had Jesus done to glorify the Father? (17:1–5)

_____

_____

(2) For whom does Jesus show the greatest concern in this prayer? Why? (17:6–19)

_____

_____

(3) What specifically does He ask for them? (17:11, 13, 15, 17)

_____

_____

_____

_____

(4) How did Jesus sanctify Himself? (17:19)

_____

_____

(5) How did He envision the world hearing the Gospel? (17:18, 20)

_____

_____

(6) How does He think of unity among the redeemed? (17:21–23)

_____

_____

(7) How many times does a form of the word "give" occur in these 26 verses? ——What does this suggest to you about the Christian life?

_____

_____

_____

16. In view of your oneness in Christ, what should you do one for another in the church?

(1) James 5:16 _____

(2) Hebrews 3:13 _____

(3) Galatians 6:2 _____

(4) 1 Thessalonians 4:18 _____

17. How should you feel toward new Christians in the church? 1 Thessalonians 2:7, 8 (Galatians 4:19)

_____

_____

18. As a goal for those you are helping, sum up Paul's objective in Colossians 1:25–29.

_____

_____

_____

19. What is the best way to develop strong Christian leadership in the church? John 13:15; 1 Corinthians 11:1

_____

_____

20. Read the farewell message of Paul to the Ephesian elders in Acts 20:17–36. Note three qualities of his example among them which challenge your commitment.

_____

_____

_____

_____

MAKE YOUR
OWN APPLICATION . . .

Looking at your life, make a mental reservation of how many people you have helped to Christ this past year, and how many of these in turn are now bearing fruit. Then list several definite ways in which you believe that your witness for Christ can be more productive for His glory.

_____

_____

_____

_____

_____

_____

_____

Memorize . . . Romans 14:8 and John 17:19

CONGRATULATIONS!

You deserve commendation for completing these lessons. It was no easy task. Working through the study has demonstrated a beautiful desire and ability to search the Scripture and let the Spirit apply to your heart the Word of truth.

If you would like to continue a directed program on a more advanced level, you might like the devotional Bible study entitled *Written In Blood.* Tracing blood-stained footprints through the Bible, it helps you see the central theme of God's redemptive revelation, and to appreciate anew that what the blood of Christ accomplished for you, the Spirit of Christ now effects in you.

Or if you would like to pursue an action-orientated study in the personal evangelism of Jesus, get into *They Meet The Master.* This in-depth approach encourages you to learn how to confront persons with the Gospel.

While growing in your personal devotion, do not forget those around you who may need your strength. Seek them out, and share what God has given to you.

Whatever you do, keep your spiritual life open-ended toward heaven. There is more to be discovered about the life which is yours in Christ. Find it! Believe it! Live in its power and glory! It is all there for you in the Holy Scripture.

NEVER STOP LEARNING

SUGGESTIONS FOR DAILY ABIDING

1. Offer yourself fully to Christ anew each morning, breathing this prayer as you awake: "Lord Jesus, I am Thine, Live Thy life through me today."

2. Thank Him for filling you afresh with His Spirit, and often during the day express to Him your praise for His faithfulness.

3. Take time to wait before Him in earnest prayer and reverent reading of the Scripture.

4. Mediate in your quiet moments upon the fact of His indwelling Presence, realizing that the Spirit of God Himself, the Holy Spirit, occupies your body, mind, and soul.

5. Confess to Him instantly any un-Christlike actions or attitudes which the Spirit reveals to you, and accept His cleansing with thanksgiving.

6. Be honest with all men, speak the truth fearlessly, and desire only God's approval.

7. Obey completely the leading of the Spirit, knowing that He never makes a mistake.

8. Rejoice in your adversities, thanking God that you are counted worthy to enter into His sufferings.

9. Look with Christlike compassion to some person in need of love, and be His minister.

10. Talk about the wonderful works of God, never boasting of your holiness or accomplishments, but be always ready to speak of His.

11. Measure yourself frequently by the Perfection of Christ, and realizing the many failures, omissions, and unimproved opportunities for service which you have unconsciously permitted, resolve to draw closer to Him as He gives you more grace.

12. Commit your way unto the Lord when the day is over, thanking Him for His all-sufficient grace, and close your eyes in the glorious confidence of abiding in Him when you awake.

... About the Author

Robert E. Coleman is the McCreless Professor of Evangelism at Asbury Theological Seminary, and also serves as president of Christian Outreach. His Bible study and discipline training books are used around the world in forty languages. He is a graduate of Southwestern University in Texas, Asbury Theological Seminary, Princeton Theological Seminary, and the University of Iowa, from which he received the Doctor of Philosophy Degree.